Affective

Jacob's Ladder

Grade 2

Reading Comprehension Program

Advanced Reading Curriculum for Social and Emotional Learning

Student Workbook

Picture Books, Short Stories, and Media, Part II

Student Name: _____

Teacher: _____

Tamra Stambaugh, Ph.D., and Joyce VanTassel-Baska, Ed.D.

Affective

Jacob's Ladder

Reading Comprehension Program

Advanced Reading Curriculum for Social and Emotional Learning

Grade

2

Student Workbook Picture Books, Short Stories, and Media, Part II

Tamra Stambaugh, Ph.D., &
Joyce VanTassel-Baska, Ed.D.

PRUFROCK PRESS INC.
WACO, TEXAS

Prufrock Press Inc.
P.O. Box 8813
Waco, TX 76714-8813
Phone: (800) 998-2208
Fax: (800) 240-0333
http://www.prufrock.com

Table of Contents

Huge Domino Screenlink!

By Dynamic Domino

View Dynamic Domino's video "Huge Domino Screenlink!" at https://www.youtube.com/watch?v=NwqYOLQF_z0.

HUGE DOMINO SCREENLINK!

Creating a Plan for Management

J3   From your list of ideas in the previous rung, select two ideas that you will practice to keep from letting everything in your life fall like dominoes when something you don't like or that doesn't go your way happens. Add the names of two people you will explain your ideas to so that they can help you with your strategy. What would you tell them? Make a list of key points.

_____

_____

_____

_____

_____

_____

_____

_____

Applying Stress Control Techniques

J2   What could be done in the video to stop the dominoes from falling? When something bad happens, how might you stop the domino effect in your life? Brainstorm a list of at least 10 things you could do to stop the dominoes from falling in a negative way.

_____

_____

_____

_____

_____

_____

_____

_____

_____

_____

Identifying Conditions/Situations That Cause Stress

J1 Sometimes people will compare dominoes falling to life events when one action causes a chain of other actions. For example, have you ever had a late start to school? What happens? First you wake up late, then you forget to grab your backpack because you are in a hurry, and then you are late to school. You miss being line leader, don't have your homework to turn in, and eventually get upset and melt down. That's a domino effect. One action causes a series of other actions. (*Note.* Usually a domino effect refers to a chain of negative events, but there can be positive domino effects, too.)

Think about a time when you were upset or having a bad day. How did an event or even your reaction to an event set off a domino effect? Draw a story map of six panels to show how one event or reaction sets off a series of other events such that you might feel like everything is falling really fast and you can't control what's happening. Use a separate sheet of paper if needed.

If at First You Don't Succeed

By Jungle Beat

View Jungle Beat's video "If at First You Don't Succeed" at https://www.youtube.com/watch?v=zitSpLHQ9CQ.

IF AT FIRST YOU DON'T SUCCEED

Demonstrating High-Level Performance in a Given Area

L3 If you were to make a list of what it takes to be successful, based on lessons learned from the video and your life, what would you say? Write a short slogan that could be used in a commercial or tweet to explain what it takes to succeed when things get challenging. Be prepared to share with others why you chose this advice, based on personal experiences and the experiences of Trunk.

_____

_____

_____

_____

_____

_____

_____

_____

Applying Learning to Practice

L2 1. Even though it might have been easy to give up, why do you think Trunk kept trying? What events do you think made him persevere?

_____

_____

_____

_____

_____

_____

_____

2. What is a time when you felt like giving up but kept trying? What events or personal characteristics helped you succeed?

_____

_____

_____

_____

_____

_____

_____

_____

_____

Recognizing Internal and External Factors That Promote Talent Development

L1 What personal characteristics did Trunk, the elephant in the video, use to make himself successful? Make a list and indicate if you do or do not have those or similar traits.

Personal Characteristics of Trunk	Your Trait

The Day the Crayons Quit

By Drew Daywalt

Duncan's crayons have quit! Duncan just wants to color, but all of his crayons are gone. Purple Crayon is mad that Duncan doesn't color inside the lines, Orange and Yellow are not speaking to each other, and Black wants to be used for more than outlines. What can Duncan do?

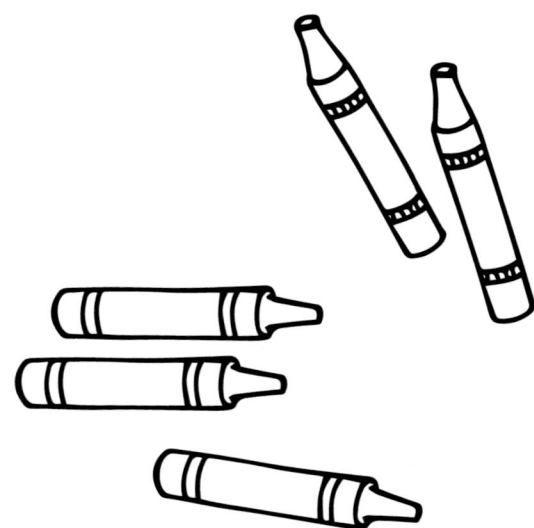

THE DAY THE CRAYONS QUIT

Collaborating With Others

I3   1. How does listening to everyone's ideas before you make a decision create a more beautiful picture, as suggested in the story? What is a way you can work together with someone else to create a better product than you could have on your own?

_____

_____

_____

_____

_____

_____

_____

_____

2. Work with a partner to create a six-panel story with pictures that illustrate how there is beauty in not being perfect.

Communicating and Responding to Others

I2   What might have happened if Duncan ignored the crayons that were not his favorite or that were overworked? Explain to a partner why it is important to consider several different people's perspectives instead of just one. Name three benefits from considering multiple perspectives in your life.

_____

_____

_____

_____

_____

_____

_____

_____

Understanding Others' Needs and Values

I1   How did each crayon express their emotions in a useful way that helped Duncan understand what each was feeling? What patterns did you notice about each crayon's comments? Was their level of communication effective? Why or why not? Use a two-column chart to organize your thoughts. Rate each crayon's level of effectiveness from 1–3, 3 being highly effective.

Patterns of Crayon Communication	Level of Effectiveness
	1 2 3
	1 2 3
	1 2 3

The Adventures of Beekle:
The Unimaginary Friend

By Dan Santat

Read the book, or view the read aloud by the author available at https://www.youtube.com/watch?v=g29lOWkAKjQ.

THE ADVENTURES OF BEEKLE: THE UNIMAGINARY FRIEND

Engaging in Productive Risk-Taking

G3 Create a two-column chart. In the first column, make a list of what it takes to make a friend. In the second column, make a list of what it takes to be a good friend. Circle at least two ideas (one from each column) that you will practice in the next week.

What It Takes to Make a Good Friend	What It Takes to Be a Good Friend

Considering Multiple Perspectives

G2 1. What are some examples of ways Beekle and his new friend considered what each other wanted or needed as part of being a good friend? Cite at least three examples.

_____

_____

_____

_____

_____

_____

_____

_____

2. What might happen if Beekle and his new friend did not consider each other's perspectives or needs as part of their new friendship?

_____

_____

_____

_____

_____

_____

_____

_____

_____

Identifying and Calculating Risks

G1 1. What risks did Beekle take to find a new friend? What is the hardest or riskiest part of making friends for you? How might you overcome or modify those risks?

_____

_____

_____

_____

_____

_____

_____

2. Write a tweet that speaks of the risks of making new friends but also offers ideas about how to overcome them.

_____

_____

_____

_____

_____

_____

_____

Pip

Directed by Bruno Simões

View the short film entitled *Pip* available at https://www.youtube.com/watch?v=07d2dXHYb94.

PIP

Demonstrating High-Level Performance in a Given Area

L3 Use at least three of the following words in sentence that makes a true statement about how someone develops talent: *try, fail, practice, succeed, learn, strength, barriers*. Your statement should be true in your life and in the video.

_____

_____

_____

_____

_____

_____

Applying Learning to Practice

L2 How did Pip use his failures and strengths to develop his talents?

When you fail or mess up, how is your reaction the same as or different from Pip's? Create a Venn diagram to compare each of your responses. Use a separate sheet of paper if necessary.

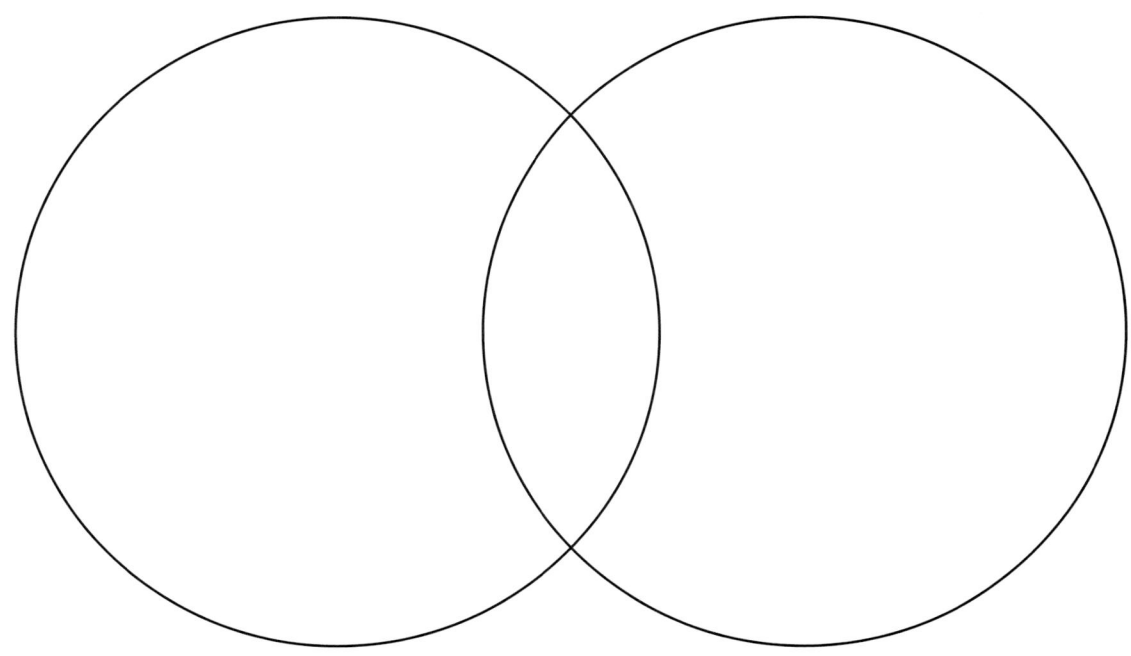

Recognizing Internal and External Factors That Promote Talent Development

L1 What are Pip's greatest assets and strengths? What were his biggest barriers? Make a list of each.

Strengths	Barriers

The Ant and the Dove

By Aesop

A thirsty ant crawled to the edge of the river to quench its thirst. The rapidly moving stream snatched the ant as it rushed by and almost drowned it. A white dove sitting on a tree plucked a leaf and let it fall into the stream close to him. The ant climbed on the leaf and floated to safety on the bank of the river. Not long after this event, a hunter came and stood under the same tree from which the dove had watched the struggling ant. The hunter sighted the dove and drew his bow to pierce his target. The ant, perceiving his plan, stung him on his foot. The hunter cried out in pain and dropped his bow. The noise made the dove fly away.

Moral: One good turn deserves another.

THE ANT AND THE DOVE

Collaborating With Others

I3 1. What are your strengths and assets? How do you show kindness to others? Chart your responses.

Strengths/Assets	How Might They Be Used for Kindness to Others?

2. Create a fable that demonstrates how creatures who are different can benefit from collaborating with each other, using their unique assets to make it happen. Use a separate sheet of paper.

Communicating and Responding to Others

I2 The fable also shows how different creatures are able to be kind in different ways. Given the characteristics of the creatures in the fable, what are the communication tools that allow them to show kindness to others?

Character	Communication Tool
The Dove	
The Hunter	
The Ant	

Understanding Others' Needs and Values

I1   What does the phrase "quid pro quo" mean? How does the act of the ant apply? Why is it a good idea, in addition to being charitable, to return a kindness? How does the fable help you understand the position of others? What would be quid pro quo acts for the following?

- Someone gives you a present.
- Someone compliments how you look.
- Someone mows your lawn.

_____

_____

_____

_____

_____

_____

_____

_____

_____

Returning acts of kindness is different from returning acts of meanness. What is the best response to meanness? Why?

_____

_____

_____

_____

_____

_____

_____

_____

_____

Each Kindness

By Jacqueline Woodson

Read the book, or view the read aloud by the author available at https://www.youtube.com/watch?v=kj7Oc0ZoOjM.

EACH KINDNESS

Actualizing Potential to Advance a Goal

H3 Why do you want friends to be kind? How does kindness affect friendships? Why? Think about activities you have done with friends in the last week or so. Use the Venn diagram below to show the relationship of kindness to acts that promote friendships.

Write in one circle the activities you have done, and in the other circle, write the way the activities made you feel. In the middle, write what positive qualities of your friendship made you feel that way.

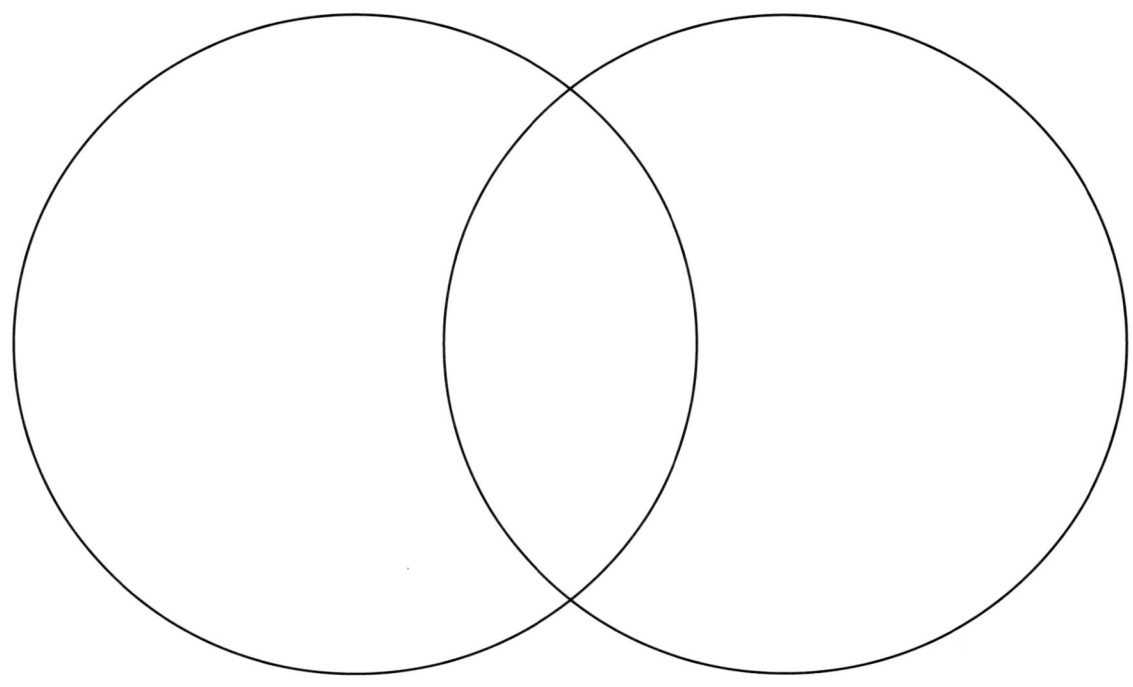

Understanding Roles and Affiliations

H2 What are the important qualities in a friend? Make a list of the important qualities in a friend, and then select your top three. Add those top three to the chart below. Explain why each of the top three are so important to you. Compare your chart with a partner's and discuss your similarities and differences.

Friend Qualities (Top 3)	Reasons for These as Priorities

Knowing Oneself

H1 What is kindness? What are examples of acts of kindness? What would have been your response to Mia when she was excluded? Write a letter to Mia, demonstrating how you would show kindness to her. Use a separate sheet of paper if needed.

_____

_____

_____

_____

_____

_____

_____

_____

_____

_____

Please visit our website at
http://www.prufrock.com

Printed in the USA

$19.95 US

ISBN-13: 978-1-64632-181-0

Affective

Jacob's Ladder

Reading Comprehension Program
Advanced Reading Curriculum for Social and Emotional Learning

Grade 2

Student Workbook

Picture Books, Short Stories, and Media, Part II

Student Name: _____

Teacher: _____

Tamra Stambaugh, Ph.D., and Joyce VanTassel-Baska, Ed.D.

Affective

Jacob's Ladder

Grade 2

Reading Comprehension Program

Advanced Reading Curriculum for Social and Emotional Learning

Student Workbook Picture Books, Short Stories, and Media, Part II

Tamra Stambaugh, Ph.D., &
Joyce VanTassel-Baska, Ed.D.

PRUFROCK PRESS INC.
WACO, TEXAS

Prufrock Press Inc.
P.O. Box 8813
Waco, TX 76714-8813
Phone: (800) 998-2208
Fax: (800) 240-0333
http://www.prufrock.com

Table of Contents

Huge Domino Screenlink!

By Dynamic Domino

View Dynamic Domino's video "Huge Domino Screenlink!" at https://www.youtube.com/watch?v=NwqYOLQF_z0.

HUGE DOMINO SCREENLINK!

Creating a Plan for Management

J3 From your list of ideas in the previous rung, select two ideas that you will practice to keep from letting everything in your life fall like dominoes when something you don't like or that doesn't go your way happens. Add the names of two people you will explain your ideas to so that they can help you with your strategy. What would you tell them? Make a list of key points.

_____

_____

_____

_____

_____

_____

_____

_____

Applying Stress Control Techniques

J2 What could be done in the video to stop the dominoes from falling? When something bad happens, how might you stop the domino effect in your life? Brainstorm a list of at least 10 things you could do to stop the dominoes from falling in a negative way.

_____

_____

_____

_____

_____

_____

_____

_____

_____

Identifying Conditions/Situations That Cause Stress

J1 Sometimes people will compare dominoes falling to life events when one action causes a chain of other actions. For example, have you ever had a late start to school? What happens? First you wake up late, then you forget to grab your backpack because you are in a hurry, and then you are late to school. You miss being line leader, don't have your homework to turn in, and eventually get upset and melt down. That's a domino effect. One action causes a series of other actions. (*Note.* Usually a domino effect refers to a chain of negative events, but there can be positive domino effects, too.)

Think about a time when you were upset or having a bad day. How did an event or even your reaction to an event set off a domino effect? Draw a story map of six panels to show how one event or reaction sets off a series of other events such that you might feel like everything is falling really fast and you can't control what's happening. Use a separate sheet of paper if needed.

If at First You Don't Succeed

By Jungle Beat

View Jungle Beat's video "If at First You Don't Succeed" at https://www.youtube.com/watch?v=zitSpLHQ9CQ.

IF AT FIRST YOU DON'T SUCCEED

Demonstrating High-Level Performance in a Given Area

L3 If you were to make a list of what it takes to be successful, based on lessons learned from the video and your life, what would you say? Write a short slogan that could be used in a commercial or tweet to explain what it takes to succeed when things get challenging. Be prepared to share with others why you chose this advice, based on personal experiences and the experiences of Trunk.

_____

_____

_____

_____

_____

_____

_____

_____

_____

Applying Learning to Practice

L2 1. Even though it might have been easy to give up, why do you think Trunk kept trying? What events do you think made him persevere?

_____

_____

_____

_____

_____

_____

_____

2. What is a time when you felt like giving up but kept trying? What events or personal characteristics helped you succeed?

_____

_____

_____

_____

_____

_____

_____

_____

_____

Recognizing Internal and External Factors That Promote Talent Development

L1 What personal characteristics did Trunk, the elephant in the video, use to make himself successful? Make a list and indicate if you do or do not have those or similar traits.

Personal Characteristics of Trunk	Your Trait

The Day the Crayons Quit

By Drew Daywalt

Duncan's crayons have quit! Duncan just wants to color, but all of his crayons are gone. Purple Crayon is mad that Duncan doesn't color inside the lines, Orange and Yellow are not speaking to each other, and Black wants to be used for more than outlines. What can Duncan do?

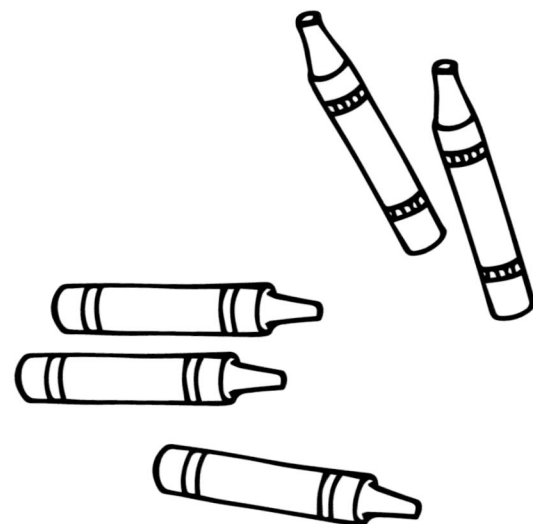

THE DAY THE CRAYONS QUIT

Collaborating With Others

I3   1. How does listening to everyone's ideas before you make a decision create a more beautiful picture, as suggested in the story? What is a way you can work together with someone else to create a better product than you could have on your own?

_____

_____

_____

_____

_____

_____

_____

_____

2. Work with a partner to create a six-panel story with pictures that illustrate how there is beauty in not being perfect.

Communicating and Responding to Others

I2   What might have happened if Duncan ignored the crayons that were not his favorite or that were overworked? Explain to a partner why it is important to consider several different people's perspectives instead of just one. Name three benefits from considering multiple perspectives in your life.

_____

_____

_____

_____

_____

_____

_____

_____

Understanding Others' Needs and Values

I1   How did each crayon express their emotions in a useful way that helped Duncan understand what each was feeling? What patterns did you notice about each crayon's comments? Was their level of communication effective? Why or why not? Use a two-column chart to organize your thoughts. Rate each crayon's level of effectiveness from 1–3, 3 being highly effective.

Patterns of Crayon Communication	Level of Effectiveness
	1 2 3
	1 2 3
	1 2 3

The Adventures of Beekle:
The Unimaginary Friend

By Dan Santat

Read the book, or view the read aloud by the author available at https://www.youtube.com/watch?v=g29lOWkAKjQ.

THE ADVENTURES OF BEEKLE: THE UNIMAGINARY FRIEND

Engaging in Productive Risk-Taking

G3 Create a two-column chart. In the first column, make a list of what it takes to make a friend. In the second column, make a list of what it takes to be a good friend. Circle at least two ideas (one from each column) that you will practice in the next week.

What It Takes to Make a Good Friend	What It Takes to Be a Good Friend

Considering Multiple Perspectives

G2 1. What are some examples of ways Beekle and his new friend considered what each other wanted or needed as part of being a good friend? Cite at least three examples.

_____

_____

_____

_____

_____

_____

_____

_____

2. What might happen if Beekle and his new friend did not consider each other's perspectives or needs as part of their new friendship?

_____

_____

_____

_____

_____

_____

_____

_____

Identifying and Calculating Risks

G1 1. What risks did Beekle take to find a new friend? What is the hardest or riskiest part of making friends for you? How might you overcome or modify those risks?

_____

_____

_____

_____

_____

_____

_____

2. Write a tweet that speaks of the risks of making new friends but also offers ideas about how to overcome them.

_____

_____

_____

_____

_____

_____

Pip

Directed by Bruno Simões

View the short film entitled *Pip* available at https://www.youtube.com/watch?v=07d2dXHYb94.

PIP

Demonstrating High-Level Performance in a Given Area

L3 Use at least three of the following words in sentence that makes a true statement about how someone develops talent: *try, fail, practice, succeed, learn, strength, barriers.* Your statement should be true in your life and in the video.

_____

_____

_____

_____

_____

_____

_____

Applying Learning to Practice

L2 How did Pip use his failures and strengths to develop his talents?

When you fail or mess up, how is your reaction the same as or different from Pip's? Create a Venn diagram to compare each of your responses. Use a separate sheet of paper if necessary.

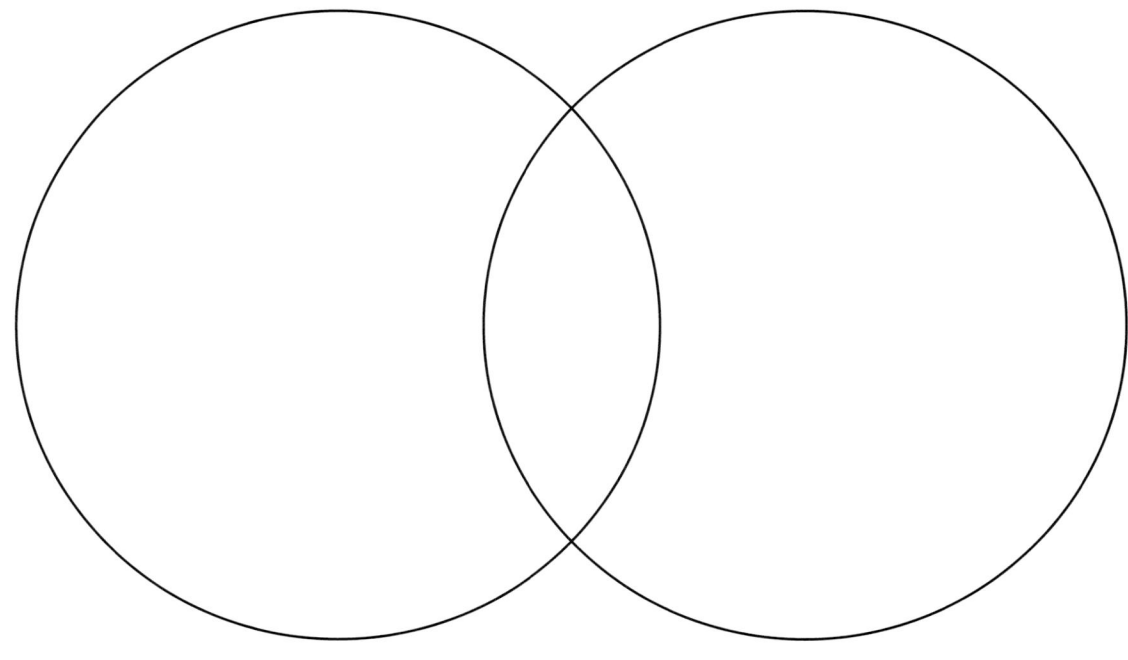

Recognizing Internal and External Factors That Promote Talent Development

L1 What are Pip's greatest assets and strengths? What were his biggest barriers? Make a list of each.

Strengths	Barriers

The Ant and the Dove

By Aesop

A thirsty ant crawled to the edge of the river to quench its thirst. The rapidly moving stream snatched the ant as it rushed by and almost drowned it. A white dove sitting on a tree plucked a leaf and let it fall into the stream close to him. The ant climbed on the leaf and floated to safety on the bank of the river. Not long after this event, a hunter came and stood under the same tree from which the dove had watched the struggling ant. The hunter sighted the dove and drew his bow to pierce his target. The ant, perceiving his plan, stung him on his foot. The hunter cried out in pain and dropped his bow. The noise made the dove fly away.

Moral: One good turn deserves another.

THE ANT AND THE DOVE

Collaborating With Others

I3 1. What are your strengths and assets? How do you show kindness to others? Chart your responses.

Strengths/Assets	How Might They Be Used for Kindness to Others?

2. Create a fable that demonstrates how creatures who are different can benefit from collaborating with each other, using their unique assets to make it happen. Use a separate sheet of paper.

Communicating and Responding to Others

I2 The fable also shows how different creatures are able to be kind in different ways. Given the characteristics of the creatures in the fable, what are the communication tools that allow them to show kindness to others?

Character	Communication Tool
The Dove	
The Hunter	
The Ant	

Understanding Others' Needs and Values

I1   What does the phrase "quid pro quo" mean? How does the act of the ant apply? Why is it a good idea, in addition to being charitable, to return a kindness? How does the fable help you understand the position of others? What would be quid pro quo acts for the following?

- Someone gives you a present.
- Someone compliments how you look.
- Someone mows your lawn.

_____

_____

_____

_____

_____

_____

_____

_____

Returning acts of kindness is different from returning acts of meanness. What is the best response to meanness? Why?

_____

_____

_____

_____

_____

_____

_____

_____

Each Kindness

By Jacqueline Woodson

Read the book, or view the read aloud by the author available at https://www.youtube.com/watch?v=kj7Oc0ZoOjM.

EACH KINDNESS

Actualizing Potential to Advance a Goal

H3 Why do you want friends to be kind? How does kindness affect friendships? Why? Think about activities you have done with friends in the last week or so. Use the Venn diagram below to show the relationship of kindness to acts that promote friendships.

Write in one circle the activities you have done, and in the other circle, write the way the activities made you feel. In the middle, write what positive qualities of your friendship made you feel that way.

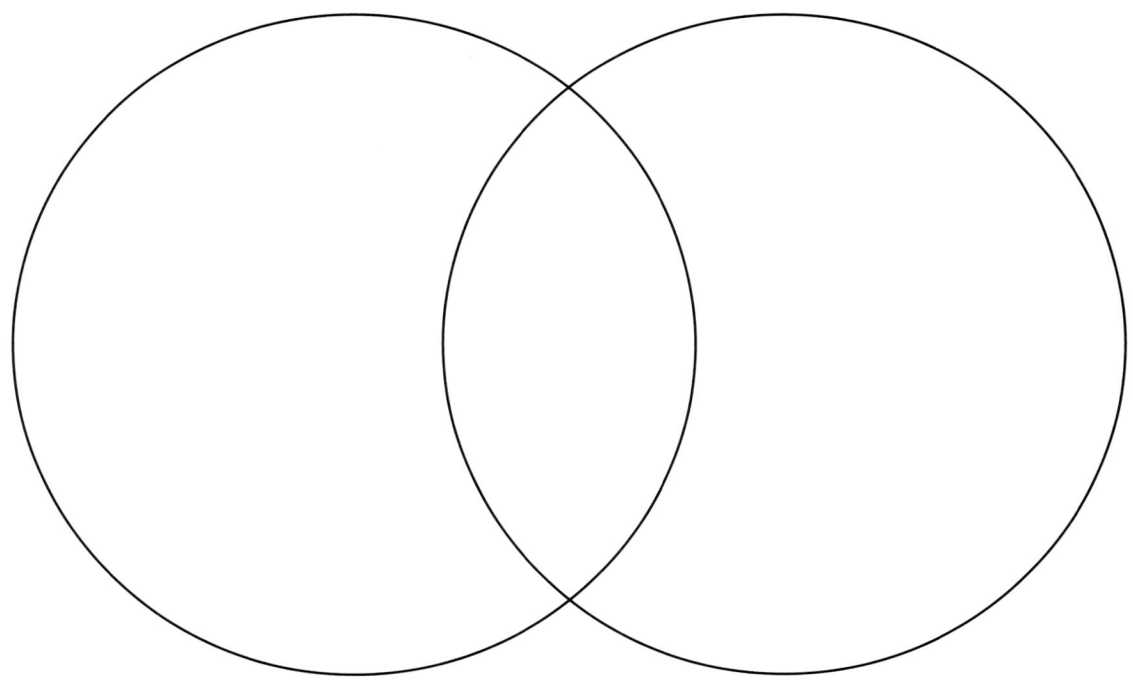

Understanding Roles and Affiliations

H2 What are the important qualities in a friend? Make a list of the important qualities in a friend, and then select your top three. Add those top three to the chart below. Explain why each of the top three are so important to you. Compare your chart with a partner's and discuss your similarities and differences.

Friend Qualities (Top 3)	Reasons for These as Priorities

Knowing Oneself

H1 What is kindness? What are examples of acts of kindness? What would have been your response to Mia when she was excluded? Write a letter to Mia, demonstrating how you would show kindness to her. Use a separate sheet of paper if needed.

_____

_____

_____

_____

_____

_____

_____

_____

_____

_____

Please visit our website at
http://www.prufrock.com

Printed in the USA

$19.95 US

ISBN-13: 978-1-64632-181-0

51995

9 781646 321810

Affective

Jacob's Ladder

Grade 2

Reading Comprehension Program
Advanced Reading Curriculum for Social and Emotional Learning

Student Workbook

Picture Books, Short Stories, and Media, Part II

Student Name: _____

Teacher: _____

Tamra Stambaugh, Ph.D., and Joyce VanTassel-Baska, Ed.D.

Affective

Jacob's Ladder

Reading Comprehension Program

Advanced Reading Curriculum for Social and Emotional Learning

Student Workbook Picture Books, Short Stories, and Media, Part II

Tamra Stambaugh, Ph.D., &
Joyce VanTassel-Baska, Ed.D.

PRUFROCK PRESS INC.
WACO, TEXAS

Prufrock Press Inc.
P.O. Box 8813
Waco, TX 76714-8813
Phone: (800) 998-2208
Fax: (800) 240-0333
http://www.prufrock.com

Table of Contents

Huge Domino Screenlink!

By Dynamic Domino

View Dynamic Domino's video "Huge Domino Screenlink!" at https://www.youtube.com/watch?v=NwqYOLQF_z0.

HUGE DOMINO SCREENLINK!

Creating a Plan for Management

J3   From your list of ideas in the previous rung, select two ideas that you will practice to keep from letting everything in your life fall like dominoes when something you don't like or that doesn't go your way happens. Add the names of two people you will explain your ideas to so that they can help you with your strategy. What would you tell them? Make a list of key points.

_____

_____

_____

_____

_____

_____

_____

_____

Applying Stress Control Techniques

J2   What could be done in the video to stop the dominoes from falling? When something bad happens, how might you stop the domino effect in your life? Brainstorm a list of at least 10 things you could do to stop the dominoes from falling in a negative way.

_____

_____

_____

_____

_____

_____

_____

_____

_____

_____

_____

Identifying Conditions/Situations That Cause Stress

J1 Sometimes people will compare dominoes falling to life events when one action causes a chain of other actions. For example, have you ever had a late start to school? What happens? First you wake up late, then you forget to grab your backpack because you are in a hurry, and then you are late to school. You miss being line leader, don't have your homework to turn in, and eventually get upset and melt down. That's a domino effect. One action causes a series of other actions. (*Note.* Usually a domino effect refers to a chain of negative events, but there can be positive domino effects, too.)

Think about a time when you were upset or having a bad day. How did an event or even your reaction to an event set off a domino effect? Draw a story map of six panels to show how one event or reaction sets off a series of other events such that you might feel like everything is falling really fast and you can't control what's happening. Use a separate sheet of paper if needed.

If at First You Don't Succeed

By Jungle Beat

View Jungle Beat's video "If at First You Don't Succeed" at https://www.youtube.com/watch?v=zitSpLHQ9CQ.

IF AT FIRST YOU DON'T SUCCEED

Demonstrating High-Level Performance in a Given Area

L3 If you were to make a list of what it takes to be successful, based on lessons learned from the video and your life, what would you say? Write a short slogan that could be used in a commercial or tweet to explain what it takes to succeed when things get challenging. Be prepared to share with others why you chose this advice, based on personal experiences and the experiences of Trunk.

_____

_____

_____

_____

_____

_____

_____

_____

Applying Learning to Practice

L2 1. Even though it might have been easy to give up, why do you think Trunk kept trying? What events do you think made him persevere?

_____

_____

_____

_____

_____

_____

_____

2. What is a time when you felt like giving up but kept trying? What events or personal characteristics helped you succeed?

_____

_____

_____

_____

_____

_____

_____

_____

_____

Recognizing Internal and External Factors That Promote Talent Development

L1 What personal characteristics did Trunk, the elephant in the video, use to make himself successful? Make a list and indicate if you do or do not have those or similar traits.

Personal Characteristics of Trunk	Your Trait

The Day the Crayons Quit

By Drew Daywalt

Duncan's crayons have quit! Duncan just wants to color, but all of his crayons are gone. Purple Crayon is mad that Duncan doesn't color inside the lines, Orange and Yellow are not speaking to each other, and Black wants to be used for more than outlines. What can Duncan do?

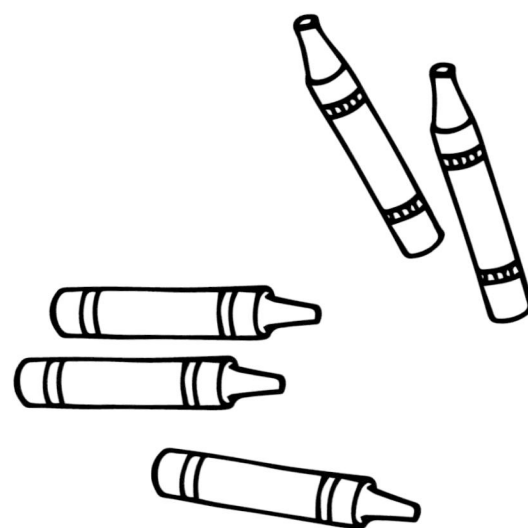

THE DAY THE CRAYONS QUIT

Collaborating With Others

I3   1.   How does listening to everyone's ideas before you make a decision create a more beautiful picture, as suggested in the story? What is a way you can work together with someone else to create a better product than you could have on your own?

_____

_____

_____

_____

_____

_____

_____

2.   Work with a partner to create a six-panel story with pictures that illustrate how there is beauty in not being perfect.

Communicating and Responding to Others

I2   What might have happened if Duncan ignored the crayons that were not his favorite or that were overworked? Explain to a partner why it is important to consider several different people's perspectives instead of just one. Name three benefits from considering multiple perspectives in your life.

_____

_____

_____

_____

_____

_____

_____

_____

_____

Understanding Others' Needs and Values

I1   How did each crayon express their emotions in a useful way that helped Duncan understand what each was feeling? What patterns did you notice about each crayon's comments? Was their level of communication effective? Why or why not? Use a two-column chart to organize your thoughts. Rate each crayon's level of effectiveness from 1–3, 3 being highly effective.

Patterns of Crayon Communication	Level of Effectiveness
	1 2 3
	1 2 3
	1 2 3

The Adventures of Beekle:
The Unimaginary Friend

By Dan Santat

Read the book, or view the read aloud by the author available at https://www.youtube.com/watch?v=g29lOWkAKjQ.

THE ADVENTURES OF BEEKLE: THE UNIMAGINARY FRIEND

Engaging in Productive Risk-Taking

G3 Create a two-column chart. In the first column, make a list of what it takes to make a friend. In the second column, make a list of what it takes to be a good friend. Circle at least two ideas (one from each column) that you will practice in the next week.

What It Takes to Make a Good Friend	What It Takes to Be a Good Friend

Considering Multiple Perspectives

G2 1. What are some examples of ways Beekle and his new friend considered what each other wanted or needed as part of being a good friend? Cite at least three examples.

_____

_____

_____

_____

_____

_____

_____

_____

2. What might happen if Beekle and his new friend did not consider each other's perspectives or needs as part of their new friendship?

_____

_____

_____

_____

_____

_____

_____

_____

_____

Identifying and Calculating Risks

G1 1. What risks did Beekle take to find a new friend? What is the hardest or riskiest part of making friends for you? How might you overcome or modify those risks?

_____

_____

_____

_____

_____

_____

_____

2. Write a tweet that speaks of the risks of making new friends but also offers ideas about how to overcome them.

_____

_____

_____

_____

_____

_____

_____

Pip

Directed by Bruno Simões

View the short film entitled *Pip* available at https://www.youtube.com/watch?v=07d2dXHYb94.

PIP

Demonstrating High-Level Performance in a Given Area

L3 Use at least three of the following words in sentence that makes a true statement about how someone develops talent: *try, fail, practice, succeed, learn, strength, barriers.* Your statement should be true in your life and in the video.

_____

_____

_____

_____

_____

_____

_____

Applying Learning to Practice

L2 How did Pip use his failures and strengths to develop his talents?

When you fail or mess up, how is your reaction the same as or different from Pip's? Create a Venn diagram to compare each of your responses. Use a separate sheet of paper if necessary.

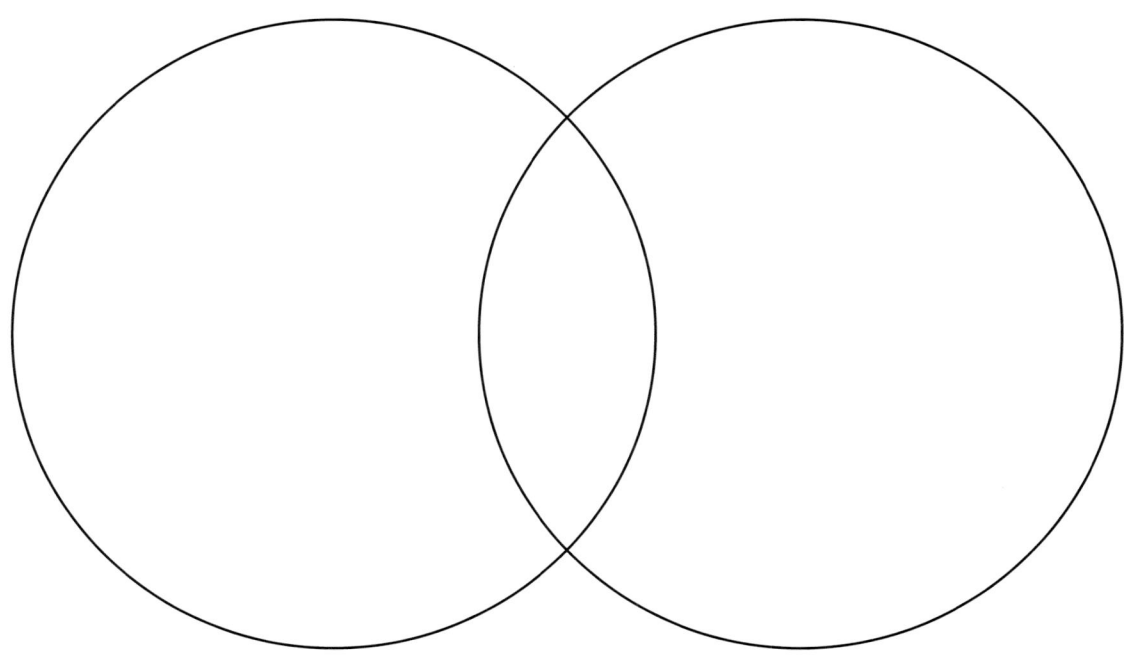

Recognizing Internal and External Factors That Promote Talent Development

L1   What are Pip's greatest assets and strengths? What were his biggest barriers? Make a list of each.

Strengths	Barriers

The Ant and the Dove

By Aesop

A thirsty ant crawled to the edge of the river to quench its thirst. The rapidly moving stream snatched the ant as it rushed by and almost drowned it. A white dove sitting on a tree plucked a leaf and let it fall into the stream close to him. The ant climbed on the leaf and floated to safety on the bank of the river. Not long after this event, a hunter came and stood under the same tree from which the dove had watched the struggling ant. The hunter sighted the dove and drew his bow to pierce his target. The ant, perceiving his plan, stung him on his foot. The hunter cried out in pain and dropped his bow. The noise made the dove fly away.

Moral: One good turn deserves another.

THE ANT AND THE DOVE

Collaborating With Others

I3   1.   What are your strengths and assets? How do you show kindness to others? Chart your responses.

Strengths/Assets	How Might They Be Used for Kindness to Others?

2.   Create a fable that demonstrates how creatures who are different can benefit from collaborating with each other, using their unique assets to make it happen. Use a separate sheet of paper.

Communicating and Responding to Others

I2   The fable also shows how different creatures are able to be kind in different ways. Given the characteristics of the creatures in the fable, what are the communication tools that allow them to show kindness to others?

Character	Communication Tool
The Dove	
The Hunter	
The Ant	

Understanding Others' Needs and Values

I1 What does the phrase "quid pro quo" mean? How does the act of the ant apply? Why is it a good idea, in addition to being charitable, to return a kindness? How does the fable help you understand the position of others? What would be quid pro quo acts for the following?

- Someone gives you a present.
- Someone compliments how you look.
- Someone mows your lawn.

_____

_____

_____

_____

_____

_____

_____

_____

Returning acts of kindness is different from returning acts of meanness. What is the best response to meanness? Why?

_____

_____

_____

_____

_____

_____

_____

_____

Each Kindness

By Jacqueline Woodson

Read the book, or view the read aloud by the author available at https://www.youtube.com/watch?v=kj7Oc0ZoOjM.

EACH KINDNESS

Actualizing Potential to Advance a Goal

H3 Why do you want friends to be kind? How does kindness affect friendships? Why? Think about activities you have done with friends in the last week or so. Use the Venn diagram below to show the relationship of kindness to acts that promote friendships.

Write in one circle the activities you have done, and in the other circle, write the way the activities made you feel. In the middle, write what positive qualities of your friendship made you feel that way.

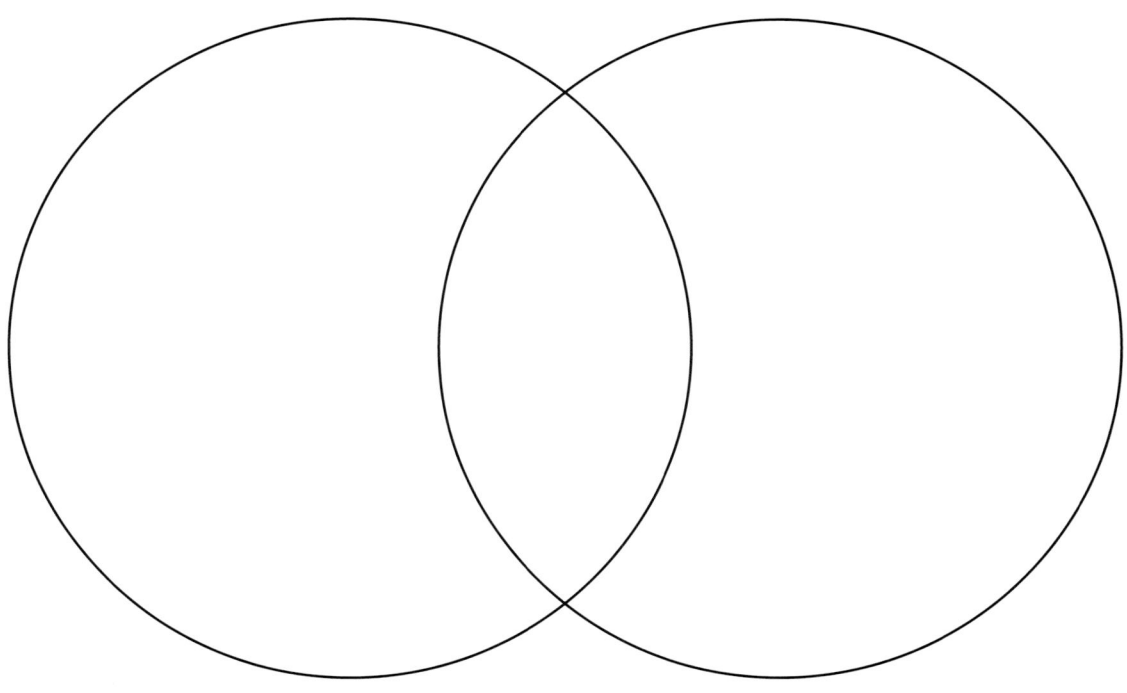

Understanding Roles and Affiliations

H2 What are the important qualities in a friend? Make a list of the important qualities in a friend, and then select your top three. Add those top three to the chart below. Explain why each of the top three are so important to you. Compare your chart with a partner's and discuss your similarities and differences.

Friend Qualities (Top 3)	Reasons for These as Priorities

Knowing Oneself

H1 What is kindness? What are examples of acts of kindness? What would have been your response to Mia when she was excluded? Write a letter to Mia, demonstrating how you would show kindness to her. Use a separate sheet of paper if needed.

_____

_____

_____

_____

_____

_____

_____

_____

_____

_____

PRUFROCK
PRESS INC.™

Please visit our website at
http://www.prufrock.com

Printed in the USA

$19.95 US

ISBN-13: 978-1-64632-181-0
51995

9 781646 321810

Affective

Jacob's Ladder

Grade 2

Reading Comprehension Program
Advanced Reading Curriculum for Social and Emotional Learning

Student Workbook

Picture Books, Short Stories, and Media, Part II

Student Name: _____

Teacher: _____

Tamra Stambaugh, Ph.D., and Joyce VanTassel-Baska, Ed.D.

Affective

Jacob's Ladder

Grade 2

Reading Comprehension Program

Advanced Reading Curriculum for Social and Emotional Learning

Student Workbook Picture Books, Short Stories, and Media, Part II

Tamra Stambaugh, Ph.D., &
Joyce VanTassel-Baska, Ed.D.

PRUFROCK PRESS INC.
WACO, TEXAS

Prufrock Press Inc.
P.O. Box 8813
Waco, TX 76714-8813
Phone: (800) 998-2208
Fax: (800) 240-0333
http://www.prufrock.com

Table of Contents

Huge Domino Screenlink!

By Dynamic Domino

View Dynamic Domino's video "Huge Domino Screenlink!" at https://www.youtube.com/watch?v=NwqYOLQF_z0.

HUGE DOMINO SCREENLINK!

Creating a Plan for Management

J3 From your list of ideas in the previous rung, select two ideas that you will practice to keep from letting everything in your life fall like dominoes when something you don't like or that doesn't go your way happens. Add the names of two people you will explain your ideas to so that they can help you with your strategy. What would you tell them? Make a list of key points.

_____

_____

_____

_____

_____

_____

_____

_____

Applying Stress Control Techniques

J2 What could be done in the video to stop the dominoes from falling? When something bad happens, how might you stop the domino effect in your life? Brainstorm a list of at least 10 things you could do to stop the dominoes from falling in a negative way.

_____

_____

_____

_____

_____

_____

_____

_____

_____

Identifying Conditions/Situations That Cause Stress

J1 Sometimes people will compare dominoes falling to life events when one action causes a chain of other actions. For example, have you ever had a late start to school? What happens? First you wake up late, then you forget to grab your backpack because you are in a hurry, and then you are late to school. You miss being line leader, don't have your homework to turn in, and eventually get upset and melt down. That's a domino effect. One action causes a series of other actions. (*Note.* Usually a domino effect refers to a chain of negative events, but there can be positive domino effects, too.)

Think about a time when you were upset or having a bad day. How did an event or even your reaction to an event set off a domino effect? Draw a story map of six panels to show how one event or reaction sets off a series of other events such that you might feel like everything is falling really fast and you can't control what's happening. Use a separate sheet of paper if needed.

If at First You Don't Succeed

By Jungle Beat

View Jungle Beat's video "If at First You Don't Succeed" at https://www.youtube.com/watch?v=zitSpLHQ9CQ.

IF AT FIRST YOU DON'T SUCCEED

Demonstrating High-Level Performance in a Given Area

L3 If you were to make a list of what it takes to be successful, based on lessons learned from the video and your life, what would you say? Write a short slogan that could be used in a commercial or tweet to explain what it takes to succeed when things get challenging. Be prepared to share with others why you chose this advice, based on personal experiences and the experiences of Trunk.

_____

_____

_____

_____

_____

_____

_____

_____

Applying Learning to Practice

L2 1. Even though it might have been easy to give up, why do you think Trunk kept trying? What events do you think made him persevere?

_____

_____

_____

_____

_____

_____

_____

2. What is a time when you felt like giving up but kept trying? What events or personal characteristics helped you succeed?

_____

_____

_____

_____

_____

_____

_____

_____

Recognizing Internal and External Factors That Promote Talent Development

L1 What personal characteristics did Trunk, the elephant in the video, use to make himself successful? Make a list and indicate if you do or do not have those or similar traits.

Personal Characteristics of Trunk	Your Trait

The Day the Crayons Quit

By Drew Daywalt

Duncan's crayons have quit! Duncan just wants to color, but all of his crayons are gone. Purple Crayon is mad that Duncan doesn't color inside the lines, Orange and Yellow are not speaking to each other, and Black wants to be used for more than outlines. What can Duncan do?

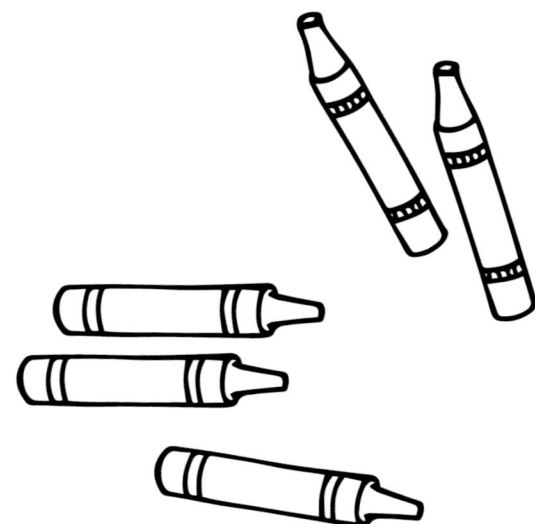

THE DAY THE CRAYONS QUIT

Collaborating With Others

I3   1.   How does listening to everyone's ideas before you make a decision create a more beautiful picture, as suggested in the story? What is a way you can work together with someone else to create a better product than you could have on your own?

_____

_____

_____

_____

_____

_____

_____

_____

2.   Work with a partner to create a six-panel story with pictures that illustrate how there is beauty in not being perfect.

Communicating and Responding to Others

I2   What might have happened if Duncan ignored the crayons that were not his favorite or that were overworked? Explain to a partner why it is important to consider several different people's perspectives instead of just one. Name three benefits from considering multiple perspectives in your life.

_____

_____

_____

_____

_____

_____

_____

_____

Understanding Others' Needs and Values

I1   How did each crayon express their emotions in a useful way that helped Duncan understand what each was feeling? What patterns did you notice about each crayon's comments? Was their level of communication effective? Why or why not? Use a two-column chart to organize your thoughts. Rate each crayon's level of effectiveness from 1–3, 3 being highly effective.

Patterns of Crayon Communication	Level of Effectiveness
	1 2 3
	1 2 3
	1 2 3

The Adventures of Beekle:
The Unimaginary Friend

By Dan Santat

Read the book, or view the read aloud by the author available at https://www.youtube.com/watch?v=g29lOWkAKjQ.

THE ADVENTURES OF BEEKLE: THE UNIMAGINARY FRIEND

Engaging in Productive Risk-Taking

G3 Create a two-column chart. In the first column, make a list of what it takes to make a friend. In the second column, make a list of what it takes to be a good friend. Circle at least two ideas (one from each column) that you will practice in the next week.

What It Takes to Make a Good Friend	What It Takes to Be a Good Friend

Considering Multiple Perspectives

G2 1. What are some examples of ways Beekle and his new friend considered what each other wanted or needed as part of being a good friend? Cite at least three examples.

_____

_____

_____

_____

_____

_____

_____

_____

2. What might happen if Beekle and his new friend did not consider each other's perspectives or needs as part of their new friendship?

_____

_____

_____

_____

_____

_____

_____

_____

Identifying and Calculating Risks

G1 1. What risks did Beekle take to find a new friend? What is the hardest or riskiest part of making friends for you? How might you overcome or modify those risks?

_____

_____

_____

_____

_____

_____

_____

2. Write a tweet that speaks of the risks of making new friends but also offers ideas about how to overcome them.

_____

_____

_____

_____

_____

_____

_____

Pip

Directed by Bruno Simões

View the short film entitled *Pip* available at https://www.youtube.com/
watch?v=07d2dXHYb94.

PIP

Demonstrating High-Level Performance in a Given Area

L3 Use at least three of the following words in sentence that makes a true statement about how someone develops talent: *try*, *fail*, *practice*, *succeed*, *learn*, *strength*, *barriers*. Your statement should be true in your life and in the video.

_____

_____

_____

_____

_____

_____

_____

Applying Learning to Practice

L2 How did Pip use his failures and strengths to develop his talents?

When you fail or mess up, how is your reaction the same as or different from Pip's? Create a Venn diagram to compare each of your responses. Use a separate sheet of paper if necessary.

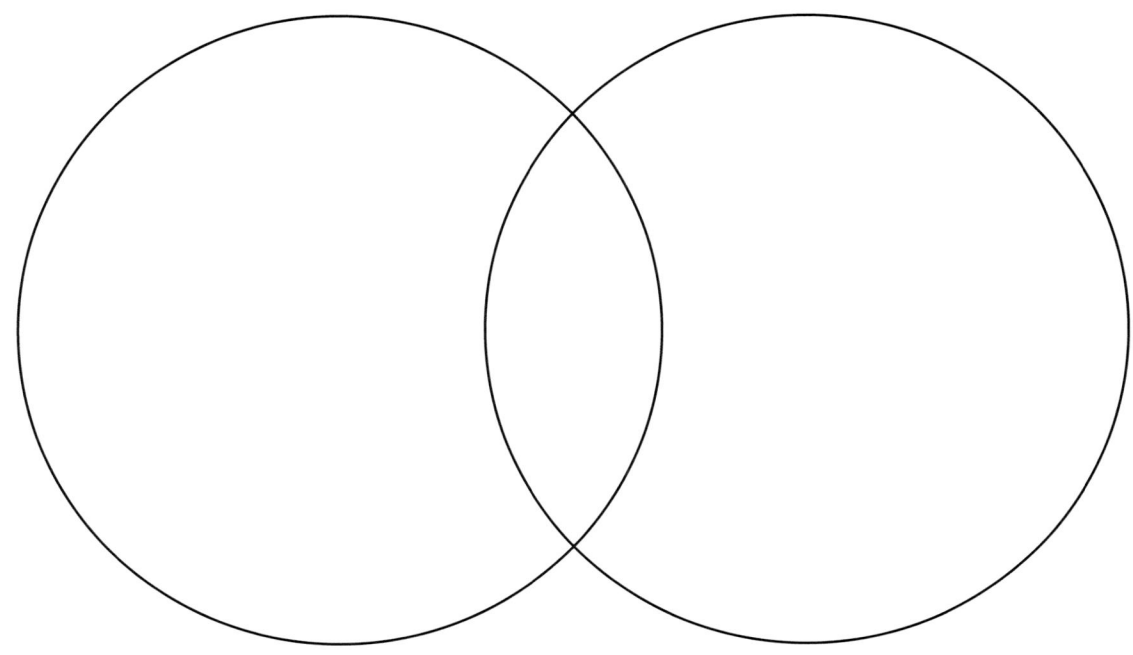

Recognizing Internal and External Factors That Promote Talent Development

L1 What are Pip's greatest assets and strengths? What were his biggest barriers? Make a list of each.

Strengths	Barriers

The Ant and the Dove

By Aesop

A thirsty ant crawled to the edge of the river to quench its thirst. The rapidly moving stream snatched the ant as it rushed by and almost drowned it. A white dove sitting on a tree plucked a leaf and let it fall into the stream close to him. The ant climbed on the leaf and floated to safety on the bank of the river. Not long after this event, a hunter came and stood under the same tree from which the dove had watched the struggling ant. The hunter sighted the dove and drew his bow to pierce his target. The ant, perceiving his plan, stung him on his foot. The hunter cried out in pain and dropped his bow. The noise made the dove fly away.

Moral: One good turn deserves another.

THE ANT AND THE DOVE

Collaborating With Others

I3   1.   What are your strengths and assets? How do you show kindness to others? Chart your responses.

Strengths/Assets	How Might They Be Used for Kindness to Others?

2.   Create a fable that demonstrates how creatures who are different can benefit from collaborating with each other, using their unique assets to make it happen. Use a separate sheet of paper.

Communicating and Responding to Others

I2   The fable also shows how different creatures are able to be kind in different ways. Given the characteristics of the creatures in the fable, what are the communication tools that allow them to show kindness to others?

Character	Communication Tool
The Dove	
The Hunter	
The Ant	

Understanding Others' Needs and Values

I1   What does the phrase "quid pro quo" mean? How does the act of the ant apply? Why is it a good idea, in addition to being charitable, to return a kindness? How does the fable help you understand the position of others? What would be quid pro quo acts for the following?

- Someone gives you a present.
- Someone compliments how you look.
- Someone mows your lawn.

_____

_____

_____

_____

_____

_____

_____

_____

Returning acts of kindness is different from returning acts of meanness. What is the best response to meanness? Why?

_____

_____

_____

_____

_____

_____

_____

_____

Each Kindness

By Jacqueline Woodson

Read the book, or view the read aloud by the author available at https://www.youtube.com/watch?v=kj7Oc0ZoOjM.

EACH KINDNESS

Actualizing Potential to Advance a Goal

H3 Why do you want friends to be kind? How does kindness affect friendships? Why? Think about activities you have done with friends in the last week or so. Use the Venn diagram below to show the relationship of kindness to acts that promote friendships.

Write in one circle the activities you have done, and in the other circle, write the way the activities made you feel. In the middle, write what positive qualities of your friendship made you feel that way.

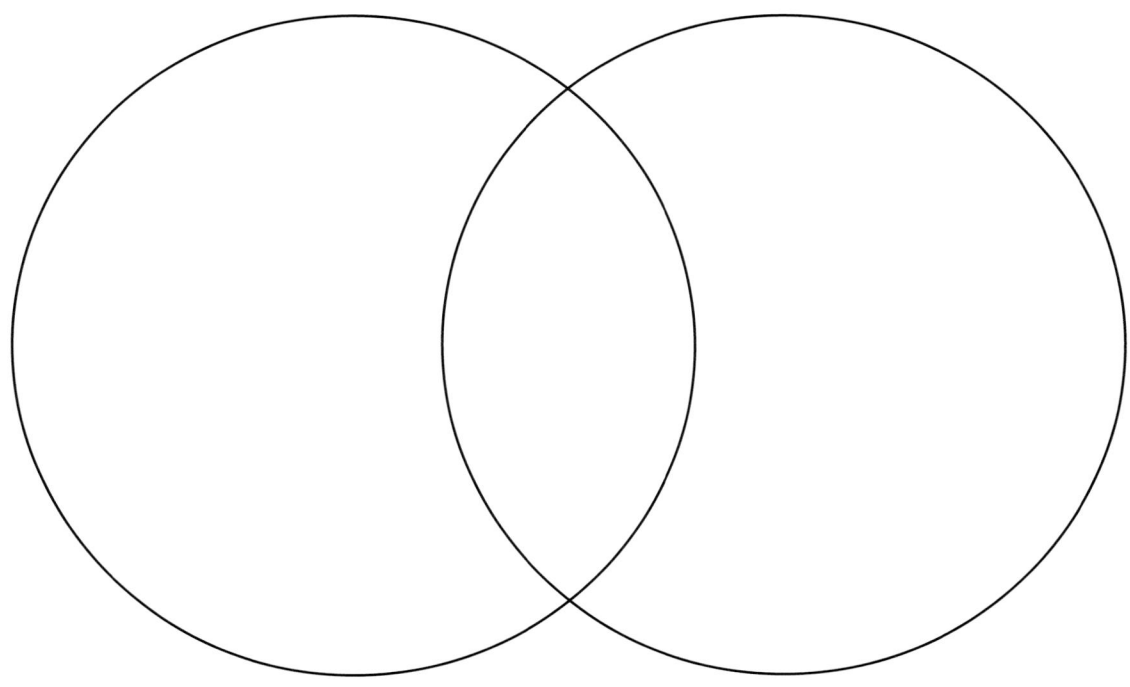

Understanding Roles and Affiliations

H2 What are the important qualities in a friend? Make a list of the important qualities in a friend, and then select your top three. Add those top three to the chart below. Explain why each of the top three are so important to you. Compare your chart with a partner's and discuss your similarities and differences.

Friend Qualities (Top 3)	Reasons for These as Priorities

Knowing Oneself

H1 What is kindness? What are examples of acts of kindness? What would have been your response to Mia when she was excluded? Write a letter to Mia, demonstrating how you would show kindness to her. Use a separate sheet of paper if needed.

_____

_____

_____

_____

_____

_____

_____

_____

_____

_____

Please visit our website at
http://www.prufrock.com

Printed in the USA

$19.95 US

ISBN-13: 978-1-64632-181-0

Affective
Jacob's Ladder
Reading Comprehension Program
Advanced Reading Curriculum for Social and Emotional Learning

Grade 2

Student Workbook

Picture Books, Short Stories, and Media, Part II

Student Name: _____

Teacher: _____

Tamra Stambaugh, Ph.D., and Joyce VanTassel-Baska, Ed.D.

Affective

Jacob's Ladder

Reading Comprehension Program

Advanced Reading Curriculum for Social and Emotional Learning

Grade 2

Student Workbook Picture Books, Short Stories, and Media, Part II

Tamra Stambaugh, Ph.D., &
Joyce VanTassel-Baska, Ed.D.

PRUFROCK PRESS INC.
WACO, TEXAS

Prufrock Press Inc.
P.O. Box 8813
Waco, TX 76714-8813
Phone: (800) 998-2208
Fax: (800) 240-0333
http://www.prufrock.com

Table of Contents

Huge Domino Screenlink!

By Dynamic Domino

View Dynamic Domino's video "Huge Domino Screenlink!" at https://www.youtube.com/watch?v=NwqYOLQF_z0.

HUGE DOMINO SCREENLINK!

Creating a Plan for Management

J3 From your list of ideas in the previous rung, select two ideas that you will practice to keep from letting everything in your life fall like dominoes when something you don't like or that doesn't go your way happens. Add the names of two people you will explain your ideas to so that they can help you with your strategy. What would you tell them? Make a list of key points.

_____

_____

_____

_____

_____

_____

_____

_____

Applying Stress Control Techniques

J2 What could be done in the video to stop the dominoes from falling? When something bad happens, how might you stop the domino effect in your life? Brainstorm a list of at least 10 things you could do to stop the dominoes from falling in a negative way.

_____

_____

_____

_____

_____

_____

_____

_____

_____

_____

Identifying Conditions/Situations That Cause Stress

J1 Sometimes people will compare dominoes falling to life events when one action causes a chain of other actions. For example, have you ever had a late start to school? What happens? First you wake up late, then you forget to grab your backpack because you are in a hurry, and then you are late to school. You miss being line leader, don't have your homework to turn in, and eventually get upset and melt down. That's a domino effect. One action causes a series of other actions. (*Note.* Usually a domino effect refers to a chain of negative events, but there can be positive domino effects, too.)

Think about a time when you were upset or having a bad day. How did an event or even your reaction to an event set off a domino effect? Draw a story map of six panels to show how one event or reaction sets off a series of other events such that you might feel like everything is falling really fast and you can't control what's happening. Use a separate sheet of paper if needed.

If at First You Don't Succeed

By Jungle Beat

View Jungle Beat's video "If at First You Don't Succeed" at https://www.youtube.com/watch?v=zitSpLHQ9CQ.

IF AT FIRST YOU DON'T SUCCEED

Demonstrating High-Level Performance in a Given Area

L3 If you were to make a list of what it takes to be successful, based on lessons learned from the video and your life, what would you say? Write a short slogan that could be used in a commercial or tweet to explain what it takes to succeed when things get challenging. Be prepared to share with others why you chose this advice, based on personal experiences and the experiences of Trunk.

_____

_____

_____

_____

_____

_____

_____

_____

Applying Learning to Practice

L2 1. Even though it might have been easy to give up, why do you think Trunk kept trying? What events do you think made him persevere?

_____

_____

_____

_____

_____

_____

_____

2. What is a time when you felt like giving up but kept trying? What events or personal characteristics helped you succeed?

_____

_____

_____

_____

_____

_____

_____

_____

_____

Recognizing Internal and External Factors That Promote Talent Development

L1 What personal characteristics did Trunk, the elephant in the video, use to make himself successful? Make a list and indicate if you do or do not have those or similar traits.

Personal Characteristics of Trunk	Your Trait

The Day the Crayons Quit

By Drew Daywalt

Duncan's crayons have quit! Duncan just wants to color, but all of his crayons are gone. Purple Crayon is mad that Duncan doesn't color inside the lines, Orange and Yellow are not speaking to each other, and Black wants to be used for more than outlines. What can Duncan do?

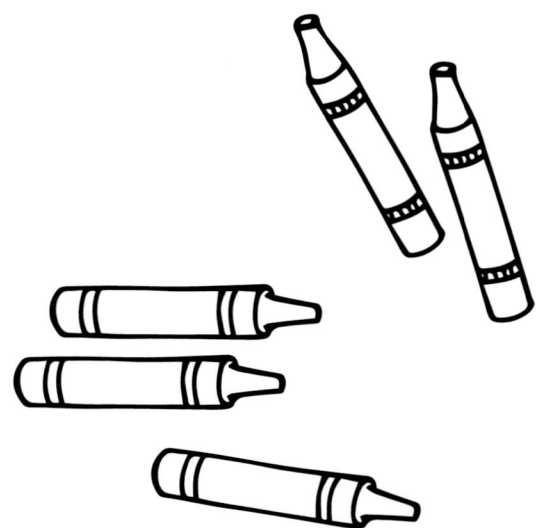

THE DAY THE CRAYONS QUIT

Collaborating With Others

I3 1. How does listening to everyone's ideas before you make a decision create a more beautiful picture, as suggested in the story? What is a way you can work together with someone else to create a better product than you could have on your own?

_____

_____

_____

_____

_____

_____

_____

_____

2. Work with a partner to create a six-panel story with pictures that illustrate how there is beauty in not being perfect.

Communicating and Responding to Others

I2   What might have happened if Duncan ignored the crayons that were not his favorite or that were overworked? Explain to a partner why it is important to consider several different people's perspectives instead of just one. Name three benefits from considering multiple perspectives in your life.

_____

_____

_____

_____

_____

_____

_____

_____

Understanding Others' Needs and Values

I1   How did each crayon express their emotions in a useful way that helped Duncan understand what each was feeling? What patterns did you notice about each crayon's comments? Was their level of communication effective? Why or why not? Use a two-column chart to organize your thoughts. Rate each crayon's level of effectiveness from 1–3, 3 being highly effective.

Patterns of Crayon Communication	Level of Effectiveness
	1 2 3
	1 2 3
	1 2 3

The Adventures of Beekle: The Unimaginary Friend

By Dan Santat

Read the book, or view the read aloud by the author available at https://www.youtube.com/watch?v=g29lOWkAKjQ.

THE ADVENTURES OF BEEKLE: THE UNIMAGINARY FRIEND

Engaging in Productive Risk-Taking

G3 Create a two-column chart. In the first column, make a list of what it takes to make a friend. In the second column, make a list of what it takes to be a good friend. Circle at least two ideas (one from each column) that you will practice in the next week.

What It Takes to Make a Good Friend	What It Takes to Be a Good Friend

Considering Multiple Perspectives

G2 1. What are some examples of ways Beekle and his new friend considered what each other wanted or needed as part of being a good friend? Cite at least three examples.

_____

_____

_____

_____

_____

_____

_____

_____

2. What might happen if Beekle and his new friend did not consider each other's perspectives or needs as part of their new friendship?

_____

_____

_____

_____

_____

_____

_____

_____

Identifying and Calculating Risks

G1 1. What risks did Beekle take to find a new friend? What is the hardest or riskiest part of making friends for you? How might you overcome or modify those risks?

_____

_____

_____

_____

_____

_____

2. Write a tweet that speaks of the risks of making new friends but also offers ideas about how to overcome them.

_____

_____

_____

_____

_____

_____

Pip
Directed by Bruno Simões

View the short film entitled *Pip* available at https://www.youtube.com/watch?v=07d2dXHYb94.

PIP

Demonstrating High-Level Performance in a Given Area

L3 Use at least three of the following words in sentence that makes a true statement about how someone develops talent: *try, fail, practice, succeed, learn, strength, barriers.* Your statement should be true in your life and in the video.

_____

_____

_____

_____

_____

_____

_____

_____

Applying Learning to Practice

L2 How did Pip use his failures and strengths to develop his talents?

When you fail or mess up, how is your reaction the same as or different from Pip's? Create a Venn diagram to compare each of your responses. Use a separate sheet of paper if necessary.

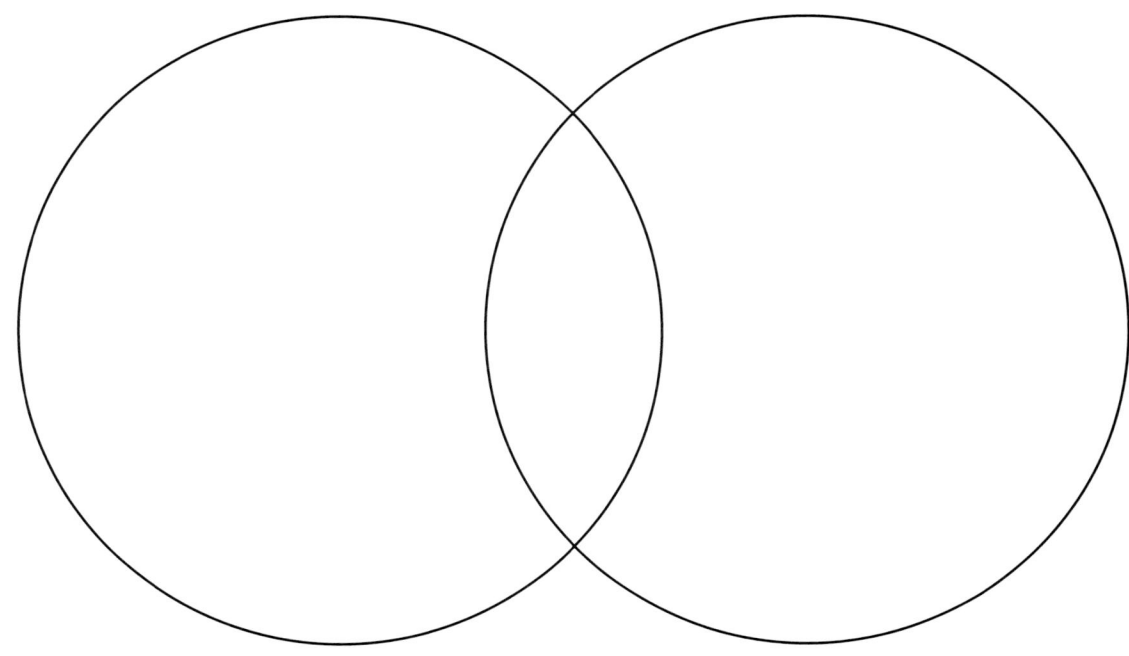

Recognizing Internal and External Factors That Promote Talent Development

L1 What are Pip's greatest assets and strengths? What were his biggest barriers? Make a list of each.

Strengths	Barriers

The Ant and the Dove

By Aesop

A thirsty ant crawled to the edge of the river to quench its thirst. The rapidly moving stream snatched the ant as it rushed by and almost drowned it. A white dove sitting on a tree plucked a leaf and let it fall into the stream close to him. The ant climbed on the leaf and floated to safety on the bank of the river. Not long after this event, a hunter came and stood under the same tree from which the dove had watched the struggling ant. The hunter sighted the dove and drew his bow to pierce his target. The ant, perceiving his plan, stung him on his foot. The hunter cried out in pain and dropped his bow. The noise made the dove fly away.

Moral: One good turn deserves another.

THE ANT AND THE DOVE

Collaborating With Others

I3 1. What are your strengths and assets? How do you show kindness to others? Chart your responses.

Strengths/Assets	How Might They Be Used for Kindness to Others?

2. Create a fable that demonstrates how creatures who are different can benefit from collaborating with each other, using their unique assets to make it happen. Use a separate sheet of paper.

Communicating and Responding to Others

I2 The fable also shows how different creatures are able to be kind in different ways. Given the characteristics of the creatures in the fable, what are the communication tools that allow them to show kindness to others?

Character	Communication Tool
The Dove	
The Hunter	
The Ant	

Understanding Others' Needs and Values

I1   What does the phrase "quid pro quo" mean? How does the act of the ant apply? Why is it a good idea, in addition to being charitable, to return a kindness? How does the fable help you understand the position of others? What would be quid pro quo acts for the following?

- Someone gives you a present.
- Someone compliments how you look.
- Someone mows your lawn.

_____

_____

_____

_____

_____

_____

_____

_____

Returning acts of kindness is different from returning acts of meanness. What is the best response to meanness? Why?

_____

_____

_____

_____

_____

_____

_____

_____

Each Kindness

By Jacqueline Woodson

Read the book, or view the read aloud by the author available at https://
www.youtube.com/watch?v=kj7Oc0ZoOjM.

EACH KINDNESS

Actualizing Potential to Advance a Goal

H3 Why do you want friends to be kind? How does kindness affect friendships? Why? Think about activities you have done with friends in the last week or so. Use the Venn diagram below to show the relationship of kindness to acts that promote friendships.

Write in one circle the activities you have done, and in the other circle, write the way the activities made you feel. In the middle, write what positive qualities of your friendship made you feel that way.

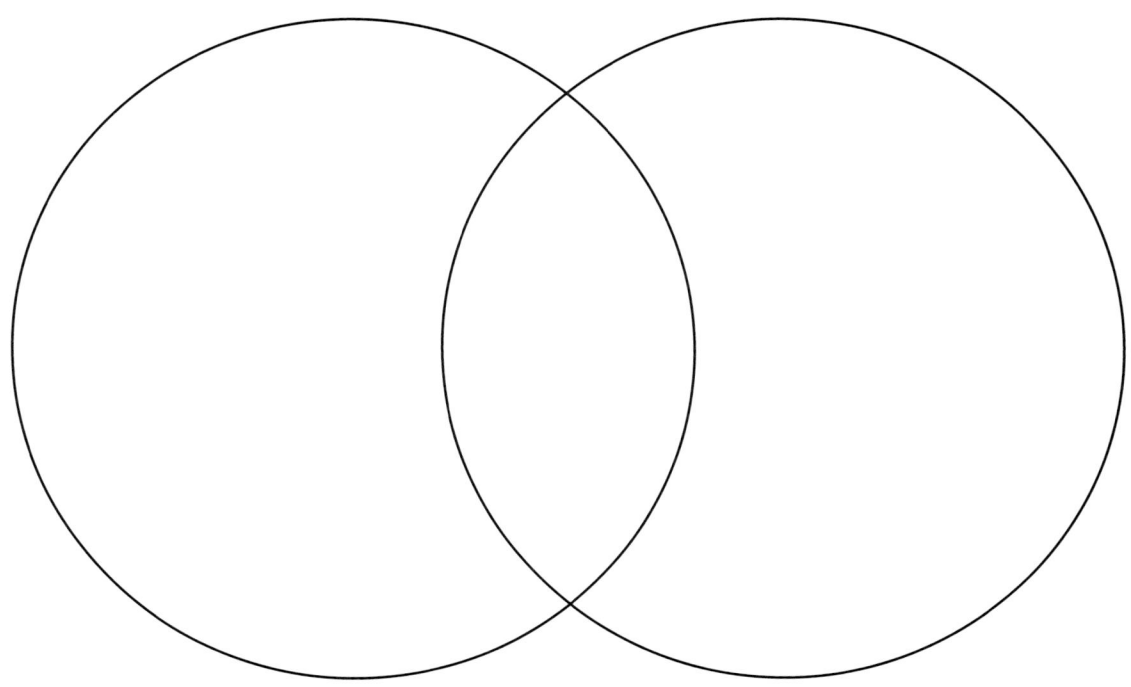

Understanding Roles and Affiliations

H2 What are the important qualities in a friend? Make a list of the important qualities in a friend, and then select your top three. Add those top three to the chart below. Explain why each of the top three are so important to you. Compare your chart with a partner's and discuss your similarities and differences.

Friend Qualities (Top 3)	Reasons for These as Priorities

Knowing Oneself

H1 What is kindness? What are examples of acts of kindness? What would have been your response to Mia when she was excluded? Write a letter to Mia, demonstrating how you would show kindness to her. Use a separate sheet of paper if needed.

_____

_____

_____

_____

_____

_____

_____

_____

_____

_____

PRUFROCK
PRESS INC.™

Please visit our website at
http://www.prufrock.com

Printed in the USA

$19.95 US

ISBN-13: 978-1-64632-181-0
51995

9 781646 321810